Spoken English Phrases

Speak English Like a Native

Book (6)

Forward

Care to have a good command of spoken English?

If you're willing to, look no further. You're in good hands now!

As a matter of fact, listening comes on top of the list when it comes to mastering a second language (this is how we learned our first language in the first place). Thus, exposing ourselves to extended periods of audible language input can never be underestimated. Besides, if we're keen to take our spoken English to the next level, we are expected to focus on the language as a whole. In other words, it pays to study the grammar, the vocabulary, the phrasal verbs, the idioms as well as the slang form of the language. Accordingly, the more engaging and effective the material is, the faster we're going to learn and develop, and here where this book comes into play.

Spoken English Phrases is a carefully selected collection of handy and commonly used phrases in English that need to be carefully considered if the learner is serious about being confident and fluent in English. In fact, there are a must-learn phrases that can never be acquired unless they are learned in practice, i.e. in conversations. For example, we say "**I owe you one**" to thank someone for helping us and as a way of saying that we will do something for them in the future. The optimal method to master such phrases is through the dialogues and interactions that are presented in a very engaging and appealing manner in this book.

I hope you will enjoy reading this book as much I enjoyed writing it...

Table of Contents

Other works by the author

Chapter 1

Expressions (1 – 10)

1. know the drill

<u>**Situation 1**</u>:

A: *I've filled out the form. What's next?*
B: **You know the drill!** *Join the line and do not move unless you're told to do so.*

<u>**Situation 2**</u>:

A: *Hey, guys! I've just learned that the boss is on an inspection tour.*
B: *No worries. When he comes around, we just put on a show and look professional, that's all.*
A: *I think we all **know the drill**. You don't have to explain it to us every time.*

<u>**Definition**</u>: to know how something is done: to be familiar with what happens or what needs to be done, without having to be told.

2. you name it

<u>**Situation 1**</u>:

A: *What kind of sports are you into these days?*
B: *Well, I enjoy windsurfing, tennis, racquetball, swimming, **you name it**.*

<u>**Situation 2**</u>:

A: *Do they offer a variety of dishes in this place?*
B: *Certainly. They serve lobster, chicken, pizza... **you name it**!*

<u>**Definition**</u>: everything a person can think of; whatever a person can think of (used to express the extent or variety of something).

3. drive safely

<u>**Situation 1**</u>:

A: *Thank you for coming to the party.* **Drive safely!**
B: *I will. Thanks for the great hospitality and the great dinner.*

<u>**Situation 2**</u>:

A: *Good-bye!*
B: *Bye!* **Drive safely.**
A: *I will.*

<u>**Definition**</u>: be careful while driving your car (more commonly used in casual speech or conversation).

4. live up to one's reputation

<u>**Situation 1**</u>:

A: *What do you think?*
B: *Great product! You guys* **live up to your reputation**.

<u>**Situation 2**</u>:

A: *Ugh-what's this disgusting object in my meal?*
B: *That's gross! This place doesn't really* **live up to its reputation** *as a five-star hotel!*

<u>**Definition**</u>: to be as good, enjoyable, etc., as people have been led to believe.

5. live up to (one's) end of the bargain

Situation 1:

A: *Mike **isn't living up to his end of the bargain**, so I am going to sue him.*
B: *Do it, and I've got your back.*

Situation 2:

A: *This smuggling stiff doesn't feel right. I'm afraid I've got to walk out of this.*
B: *You can't quit now. You have to **live up to your end of the bargain**.*

Definition: to do as was promised in an agreement or bargain; to carry through with what one agreed to do.

6. live up to something

Situation 1:

A: *Did the vacation **live up to** your expectations?*
B: *Not really. It left a lot to be desired.*

Situation 2:

A: *I've literally screwed up today's match! My team expected a lot of me, but I couldn't **live up to** their expectations.*
B: *That loss wasn't your fault. There is no need to kick yourself.*

Definition: to achieve what is expected, esp. high standards.

7. kick oneself

<u>**Situation 1**</u>:

A: *Sorry, guys. I won't be able to attend the party. I have a paper due on Tuesday and I'll **kick myself** if I don't start on it this evening.*
B: *No excuses! I'll help you with that paper so you can complete it before noon.*

<u>**Situation 2**</u>:

A: *Make sure you have the car checked before the trip. Sure, it's expensive, but you'll **kick yourself** if it breaks down on the road.*
B: *Good point. I'll take it to the garage right away!*

<u>**Definition**</u>: to be annoyed with oneself (especially for missing an opportunity) or for doing something wrong; to be angry at oneself because you do something you regret.

8. good point

<u>**Situation 1**</u>:

A: *I think we should take the Highway on our way back.*
B: *But there's a lot of traffic on that road after work.*
A: *Yeah. That's **a good point.***

<u>**Situation 2**</u>:

A: *There's no way I'll be able to complete that report on time as long as I'm not asking for help from the management.*
B: ***Good point.***

<u>**Definition**</u>: that's a good idea; that makes sense; you're right.

9. get someone through something

Situation 1:

A: *Playing video games all the time! Is that how you live?*
B: *Of course, not. It just **gets me through** the period of quarantine.*

Situation 2:

A: *Jesus! It completely slipped my mind that I have a presentation tomorrow!*
B: *Hey, take courage and study these tips to **get you through** this awkward situation.*

Definition: to make it possible for that person to deal successfully with a difficult or painful experience, and come to the end of it; to help someone to endure some experience.

10. get through to someone (1)

Situation 1:

A: *Mike is determined to quit his job, and I just don't seem to be able to **get through to him**.*
B: *Don't worry. I'll see him tonight and talk some sense into him.*

Situation 2:

A: *Bill's working around the clock these days. I can't **get through to** him that he must rest.*
B: *Bill is a smart person, and he knows what he's doing. I think he's trying to prove himself in his new job.*

Definition: to cause someone to understand or believe you.

Measure your progress

<u>**Fill in the gaps with the missing words;**</u>

1. When you leave, shut off all the lights and lock the room with the safe. You .... the drill.

2. Sally is a gifted girl. She can make anything: chairs, tables, cupboards you .... it.

3. Good night Frank and please, ... safely!

4. Great dish! This really lives up to your .... as a master chef.

5. It is about time that the administration live up to its .... of the bargain by giving its staff the pay and respect it deserves.

6. He never managed to .... up to his parents' expectations.

7. If you don't stay home and work on your paper tonight you're going to .... yourself tomorrow.

8. "A: I think we should skip school today. The weather is terrible." "B: Good ....

9. You were always there for me. You .... me through the worst times.

10. She just will not listen to me—I don't know how to get .... to her.

Answers;

1. know   2. name   3. drive   4. reputation   5. side
6. live   7. kick   8. point   9. got   10. through

Chapter 2

Expressions (11 – 20)

11. get through (to someone) (2)

<u>Situation 1</u>:

A: *Did you hear from Jack yet?*
B: *Nope, the line is busy—I can't **get through**.*

<u>Situation 2</u>:

A: *I hate dealing with the bank over the phone. It takes ages to **get through** to the right person.*
B: *So do I.*

<u>Definition</u>: to be able to reach or contact someone.

12. make one's point

<u>Situation 1</u>:

A: *We can wait until Sarah is back, but the last bus leaves in thirty minutes. This means we'll miss it.*
B: *OK, you **made your point**. Let's get moving.*

<u>Situation 2</u>:

A: *Settle down, buddy. Why is the hurry?*
B: *Unless we make the payment today, we'll be charged extra fees. Have I **made my point**?*
A: *Oh, now I get it!*

<u>Definition</u>: to explain one's opinion, idea, or point of view.

13. think ill of someone/something

Situation 1:

A: *I don't feel up to going to this event, but the manager will think I'm skipping it on purpose.*
B: *Relax! No-one will **think ill of** you if you decide not to go.*

Situation 2:

A: *You know what? I've the worst colleagues ever. All they do is find fault with me and my work.*
B: *Boy, it's no joke when people **think ill of** your work.*

Definition: to think unpleasant things about someone or something: to have a poor opinion abt someone or something.

14. think highly of someone/something

Situation 1:

A: *This math project is driving me crazy. I'm literally going nowhere despite all the research I've done!*
B: *You should ask Jessie for help. The professor always **thinks highly of** her work.*

Situation 2:

A: *You seem to be doing a good job at work. Joe. I was speaking to your boss the other day, and he **thinks very highly of** you.*
B: *Well, that's what usually happens when you put your heart into your work, doesn't it?*
A: *Without a doubt!*

Definition: to have a good, favorable, high opinion (of someone).

15. go/get nowhere

Situation 1:

A: *It came to my ears that you broke up with John, did you?*
B: *Yeah. He and I dated for a while, but it **went nowhere**.*

Situation 2:

A: *Come on, Jack. Haven't you replaced that tire already? It's hot and I'm tired and hungry.*
B: *Can you get me that wrench? We'll **get nowhere** if all you can do is complain.*

Definition: to not make any progress or achieve anything.

16. put one's heart into something

Situation 1:

A: *I can't believe that I **put my heart and soul into** this report only to have the boss reject it.*
B: *I told you; unless you follow the guidelines, you won't get anywhere.*

Situation 2:

A: *What a beautiful place! How did you manage to do that?*
B: *We **put our heart and mind into** even the smallest acts. This is our secret.*

Definition: to put all your energy and sincere effort into something; to work hard in order to do or get something.

17. overthink

Situation 1:

A: *Mike's manager thinks highly of his work. When he was in our department, he didn't use to do well though!*
B: *Weird. Probably, the change might has enabled him to relax and not* **overthink**.

Situation 2:

A: *Jesus! The boss wants me to explain what happened to the equipment.*
B: *Don't* **overthink** *the situation, or any consequences and you'll do just fine.*

Definition: to think about (something) too much in a way that is not useful.

18. you never can tell

Situation 1:

A: *I never expected those neighbors to be so rude. It's supposed to be a really good neighborhood, but* **you never can tell**, *I guess.*
B: *I'm also in shock. What's wrong with people these days?*

Situation 2:

A: *I think we need to put aside some of our income as savings. Who knows what will happen to us in the future -* **you can never tell**!
B: *Good point!*

Definition: there is no way of knowing or being certain, esp. about the future; the future is always uncertain and it is never possible to know exactly what will happen.

19. you never know

<u>**Situation 1**</u>:

A: *I don't think John will lend us the money.*
B: **You never know**. *Have you asked him?*
A. *Not yet, but I will tonight.*
B. *That'd be a good idea.*

<u>**Situation 2**</u>:

A: *I've been searching for that part for three days in a row, but I still couldn't find it.* **You never know**, *I might get lucky.*
B: *Right, don't give up. Just keep on trying.*

<u>**Definition**</u>: said to mean there is a possibility that something good might happen, even if it is slight.

20. you may well ask

<u>**Situation 1**</u>:

A: *We're keen to engage you, the locals, in our project. So,* **you may well ask**, *what's this to do with the environment? Well, it's all about raising awareness.*
B: *Good point - we can't wait to get started.*

<u>**Situation 2**</u>:

A: **You may well ask** *what happened to the car. Well, I smashed into a tree while I was parking it, that's all.*
B: *Well done, honey. Thankfully, you didn't smash into someone.*
A: *Enough of these stupid remarks. That's not funny, isn't it?*
B: *Sorry!*

<u>**Definition**</u>: (it would be very interesting to know) used for saying that it would be reasonable to ask or think something.

Measure your progress

Fill in the gaps with the missing words;

1. I kept trying to get .... to you, but all I got was a busy signal.

2. I see what you mean about hiking in this weather being dangerous- you've .... your point.

3. You must not .... ill of her because she did not love you.

4. Your boss must think .... of you if she gives you so much responsibility.

5. No wonder you're late. You'll get .... if you don't follow the instruction.

6. Come on, choir. You can sing better than that. Put your .... into it!

7. The problem was not as serious as he thought, he was just .... it

8. You never can .... what life is going to bring you.

9. I don't think I'll get the job but you .... know.

10. But why write a novel, you .... well ask, when we were aiming to make a movie?

Answers;

1. through   2. made   3. ill   4. highly   5. nowhere
6. heart   7. overthinking   8. tell   9. never   10. may

Chapter 3

Expressions (21 – 30)

21. guesswork

Situation 1:

A: *I suggest we do more research before deciding on our marketing plan. We had better not deal in rumors or* **guesswork***.*
B: *Good point! Actual data is the name of the game when it comes to marketing.*

Situation 2:

A: *Sir, you turned down my proposal. Can I know what's wrong with it?*
B: *Your conclusions were largely founded on* **guesswork***.*

Definition: the process of making a guess when you do not know all the facts; the process or results of guessing.

22. rub shoulders with

Situation 1:

A: *Bill, what's special about your job as a reporter?*
B: *Well, as a reporter I get to* **rub shoulders** *with all the big names in politics. That's a big deal for me.*

Situation 2:

A: *I heard you were* **rubbing shoulders** *with the chief officer last Saturday.*
B: *Oh, yeah. He's my cousin, all the same.*

Definition: to meet or spend time with someone socially, esp. someone important or famous.

23. hands down (1)

Situation 1:

A: *I wasn't able to attend the contest last night. Did I miss out on the fun?*
B: *Not really! As always, we won the three rounds* **hands down**.

Situation 2:

A: *Lara is a smart girl. She won the debate* **hands down**.
B: *Being smart has nothing to do with winning. She did her homework well, that's why.*

Definition: winning with ease or with little or no effort.

24. hands down (2)

Situation 1:

A: *So, did you like my mother's pastry?*
B: *This is the best pie I've ever had,* **hands down***!*

Situation 2:

A: *Who do you think is the most worthy of promotion?*
B: *Simon is* **hands down** *the best employee in my department.*

Definition: without a doubt; definitely.

25. feel cheap

Situation 1:

A: *What are you up to tomorrow evening?*
B: *I'll have my cousins around for dinner. I **feel cheap** not being able to return their invitations.*

Situation 2:

A: *Why did you leave the office all of a sudden?*
B: *I **felt cheap** and stupid, like a naughty child caught stealing.*

Definition: (slang) to have a sense of inferiority; to feel ashamed or embarrassed.

26. speak someone's language

Situation 1:

A: *Look, I know all these math problems are pretty boring. Why don't we put them aside and go out for pizza?*
B: *Oh yeah, now you're **speaking my language**!*

Situation 2:

A: *The data shows that our budget is strained because of the taxation burdens.*
B: *I can't make out a word of what you're saying. I want you **to speak my language** and tell me how can we make more profits.*

Definition: to say something that one agrees with or understands; to have similar ideas and similar ways of expressing them.

27. accidents (will) happen

Situation 1:

A: *Oh, no. I spilled the coffee on the couch! I'm really sorry. I didn't mean it!*
B: *Okay, okay. Settle down, dear,* **accidents happen***!*

Situation 2:

A: *I know that* **accidents happen***, but I still can't believe I smashed into that truck!*
B: *Don't kick yourself for that, okay? Thankfully, you're fine.*

Definition: said after an accident in order to make it seem less bad (no matter how careful you try to be, it is inevitable that some unexpected or bad events will occur).

28. overhear

Situation 1:

A: *I* **overheard** *a very funny conversation on the bus this morning. A girl was telling her friends how her cat ate her breakfast. I could hardly restrain myself from laughing out loud.*
B: *That's really funny.*

Situation 2:

A: *Sir, we* **overheard** *some customers say that they didn't really like the food.*
B: *Jesus! Where's the master chef? Go get him immediately.*

Definition: to hear what others are saying when they are not talking to you and they do not know that you are listening.

<h2 style="text-align:center">29. keep on something</h2>

<u>Situation 1</u>:

A: *I'm going to call the cops on our neighbors if those construction men **keep on** making such a racket.*
B: *No need. Look, they're almost done!*

<u>Situation 2</u>:

A: *Are we going to take a break any time soon? I feel dizzy!*
B: *I'm afraid not. We'll have to **keep on** driving while there's still daylight.*

<u>**Definition**</u>: to continue to do something.

<h2 style="text-align:center">30. keep on at someone</h2>

<u>Situation 1</u>:

A: *Hey, baldy man! Would you like a coffee?*
B: *Don't **keep on at** George about his hair or he'll get a complex.*

<u>Situation 2</u>:

A: *Her, Joe. What are you doing outside? You should be in class now!*
B: *The teacher **kept on at** me about my tattoos and I had to leave the class.*

<u>**Definition**</u>: (*British English*) to repeatedly ask or tell them something in a way that annoys them.

Measure your progress

<u>Fill in the gaps with the missing words;</u>

1. The question of why those structures were built and who built them thousands of years ago remains a matter of ....

2. He loved his job because he got to rub .... with high-powered Hollywood stars.

3. Being an experienced author, Nigel always won hands .... in any argument.

4. The pixie cut is .... down one of the most popular funky hairstyles

5. Little Tom felt .... because he'd lied to his friend.

6. I don't know what you mean by these terms. Could you please speak my .... and tell me how I can solve this missing card issue?

7. "A: I'm sorry, mommy. I didn't mean to knock over the lamp." "B: Don't worry sweetie, ... will happen."

8. They were standing near enough for us to .... their conversation.

9. No one is born a genius. Just .... on doing what you like and that itself is a talent.

10. I will mend the lamp just don't keep on .... me about it!

Answers;

1. guesswork   2. shoulders   3. down   4. hands   5. cheap
6. language   7. accidents   8. overhear   9. keep   10. at

Chapter 4

Expressions (31 – 40)

31. it's unlike you

<u>Situation 1</u>:

A: *You're not joking today, buddy.* **It's unlike you**!
B: *I'm concerned about my sister. She's in hospital.*

<u>Situation 2</u>:

A: **It's unlike you** *to be quiet - is something wrong?*
B: *No. I've a lot of stuff to do today. I need to concentrate.*

<u>Definition</u>: the way you are behaving right now is not how you usually behave.

32. Says who?

<u>Situation 1</u>:

A (math teacher): *History is a useless subject.*
B (history teacher): *Oh, really?* **Says who?**

<u>Situation 2</u>:

A: *Hey, Joe. You owe me some money.*
B: **Say who?**

<u>Definition</u>: "I disagree with what you just said (used when you are arguing with someone, to show that you do not accept or agree with what they say).

33. hands-off approach

Situation 1:

A: *I observed that Steve takes a **hands-off approach** when it comes to raising his children.*
B: *That's right. He lets them grow on their own and learn lessons for themselves.*

Situation 2:

A: *The players are showing measurable improvement in their performance.*
B: *That's right. It's all thanks to the new coach. He takes a **hands-off** approach and lets everyone functions on their own.*

Definition: a way of organizing or dealing with something without being personally or directly involved in it.

34. first-hand experience

Situation 1:

A: *Good for you, Bill. You saved the man's life! How did you learn that?*
B: *I learned life sustaining measures from **first-hand experience**.*

Situation 2:

A: *The students are so thrilled about the mid-term break trip.*
B: *I bet they are. They'll get direct and **first-hand experience** of viewing wildlife.*

Definition: experience that is gained or learned directly, rather than from other people or from books.

35. at hand

Situation 1:

A: *Let's talk about the actual problems we have* **at hand** *and worry about financial matters later.*
B: *Alright then. I'll speak your language and say that we're losing money because our product needs an urgent update – it's simply outdated!*

Situation 2:

A: *I like to have my tools near* **at hand** *when I'm working.*
B: *So do I. That's a perfect recipe to increase productivity.*

Definition: 1. available or happening now 2. close or nearby.

36. get to do something

Situation 1:

A: *Sally hasn't been around for a while! Have you seen her recently?*
B: *I never* **get to see** *her now that she's moved to another neighborhood.*

Situation 2:

A: *I'd like to* **get to know** *you better – could we have dinner sometime?*
B: *Sure, call round to see me anytime.*

Definition: to have an opportunity to do something; to be given the permission or the opportunity to do something.

37. get someone to do something

Situation 1:

A: *John, please don't miss Sally's birthday. You'll disappoint her if you do.*
B: *I will. Actually, I've got an important meeting, but I'll try to **get them to excuse** me from it.*

Situation 2:

A: *The washing machine isn't working well. We need to **get someone to** fix it.*
B: *I'll **get Tom to have** a look at it tomorrow.*

Definition: to ask, convince or force someone to do something.

38. get to something

Situation 1:

A: *Let me finish sorting out the clothes and then I'll **get to the cleaning**.*
B: *I'll make you a coffee in the meantime.*
A: *Thanks, honey. Please do.*

Situation 2:

A: *Peter, you submitted your assignment two days late, that's unlike you!*
B: *Excuse me, sir. I couldn't **get to the assignment** until Sunday because I had to help my dad last week.*

Definition: to start on [doing] something; to begin doing something.

39. get to someone (1)

Situation 1:

A: *Hey, George. Maya says she was evicted from her apartment and needs help.*
B: *I'll **get to her** on the telephone and tell her what to do.*

Situation 2:

A: *Excuse me, can anyone tell me how much this T-shirt is?*
B: *Yes, sir. I will **get to** you in a moment. Please be patient.*

Definition: to be able to deal with someone; to manage to communicate with or contact someone.

40. get to someone (2)

Situation 1:

A: *Mike keeps finding fault with everything I do. He's really irritating.*
B: *I know he's annoying, but you shouldn't let him **get to you**.*

Situation 2:

A: *I'm under a lot of pressure at work, and sometimes it **gets to me** a bit.*
B: *All you need is an extended a break. Don't let things **get to you**.*

Definition: to bother or annoy someone.

Measure your progress

Fill in the gaps with the missing words;

1. Leave the girl alone, Bill. It's .... you to keep on at her.

2. "A: You can't show those files to the boss!" "B: Oh, really? Says ....?"

3. Paul has a .... -off approach of management. All his team are happy.

4. My first-............................... experience of English enabled me to get the job easily.

5. Soon school will end and the vacation will be at ....

6. After a time you .... to realize that these things don't matter.

7. If your customers are serious, you must get them .... come over here.

8. We will .... to the question of where you will spend the night after we discuss whether you will leave or not.

9. Fill out this form and I'll .... to you in a minute.

10. As much as I enjoy the spring, it's not long until my allergies start to .... to me.

Answers;

1. unlike   2. who   3. hands   4. hand   5. hand
6. get   7. to   8. get   9. get   10. get

Chapter 5

Expressions (41 – 50)

<h3 style="text-align:center">41. get to somewhere</h3>

<u>Situation 1</u>:

A: *How do I **get to** the shoe store?*
B: *Take the first left and go through the second door on the right.*

<u>Situation 2</u>:

A: *What time does this train **get to** New York?*
B: *At seven p.m.*

<u>Definition</u>: to arrive.

<h3 style="text-align:center">42. get somewhere</h3>

<u>Situation 1</u>:

A: *You finally allowed your assistant to sign the contract on your behalf? OK, now we're **getting somewhere**.*
B: *Yeah, we have to show some resilience o keep the work going smoothly.*

<u>Situation 2</u>:

A: *Wake up, Joe. We must pay the price in order to **get somewhere** in life – siting back and dreaming won't get you anywhere.*
B: *What kind of price?*
A: *Effort, commitment and perseverance.*

<u>Definition</u>: to make progress

<h3 align="center">43. the heart of the matter</h3>

<u>Situation 1</u>:

A: *This was a great evening. And now we come to **the heart of the matter**. Who is going to pay for all this?*
B: *I'm the one who's invited all of you, guys. I'll take care of the bill.*
A: *Please don't. I think we had better go Dutch.*

<u>Situation 2</u>:

A: *We're able to take the project on our own, but here's **the heart of the matter**. How can we secure the necessary machines?*
B: *Leave this to me. I know many dealers downtown who rent out construction equipment.*

<u>Definition</u>: the most central and important part of a situation, problem, etc.

<h3 align="center">44. get/come to the point</h3>

<u>Situation 1</u>:

A: *Guys, we've been talking about irrelevant stuff for a long time. I wish we could **come to the point**.*
B: *What do you mean?*
A: *Well, we're here basically to discuss the math project not the picnic arrangement!*

<u>Situation 2</u>:

A: *I feel this isn't the right time for us to get married. I mean we're still young and still have a long way to go before we make such a decision.*
B: *Jessie, will you stop waffling and **get to the point**?*
A: *OK. I'm simply not ready for marriage now.*

<u>Definition</u>: to reach the main or most important idea or part of something.

45. waffle

Situation 1:

A: *Did you get through to William?*
B: *Yeah, but he kept **waffling** and finding excuses not to close the deal.*
A: *You need to be patient with him. I know he's a waffler.*

Situation 2:

A: *What did you overhear? Will you stop **waffling** and tell me already?*
B: *The boss will lay off half of our team. Unfortunately, both of us are fired.*
A: *That doesn't strike me as surprising. I knew they'd take such a step and prepared a backup plan already.*

Definition: to be indecisive; to fail to make up one's mind; to keep changing your decisions about something so that no clear decision is made.

46. strike someone as something

Situation 1:

A: *It **strikes me as very odd** that a family should be split into fighting factions for the sake of some inherited money!*
B: *Some money! We're talking about millions, man.*

Situation 2:

A: *Mary was complaining all the time about everything. Her behavior **struck me as childish**.*
B: *Typical Mary. She just likes to be the center of attention.*

Definition: to cause (someone) to think about someone or something in a particular way.

47. the center of attention

<u>Situation 1</u>:

A: *After winning that prize, I found myself **the center of attention** wherever I went.*
B: *This doesn't strike me as strange. People are usually drawn to the ones who are clever and successful.*

<u>Situation 2</u>:

A: *Bob doesn't want to join the event because he doesn't like to be **the center of attention**.*
B: *Weird! He is very different from his flamboyant father.*

<u>**Definition**</u>: the person, thing, or area that everyone nearby notices and watches.

48. hand something down

<u>Situation 1</u>:

A: *I like this stew. I've never eaten something like this.*
B: *Well, this is an exclusive family recipe that had been **handed down** from generation to generation in our family.*

<u>Situation 2</u>:

A: *Do you have to wear your elder bothers' clothes like me?*
B: *Of course, it's a tradition in our family that clothes should be **handed down** from one to the next.*

<u>**Definition**</u>: to give or teach something to a younger member of your family; to pass traditions from older people to younger ones.

49. hand it over

Situation 1:

A: *Whose is this box of biscuits?*
B: *It's mine.* **Hand it over!**

Situation 2:

A: *Please* **hand this over** *to your parents to sign it and bring it back tomorrow.*
B: *Will do. Thanks for your help.*

Definition: give it to me.

50. wash one's hand of

Situation 1:

A: *Are you still mediating between Bob and Dave?*
B: *No, not anymore. I've* **washed my hands of** *the whole matter.*

Situation 2:

A: *Tom's parents* **washed their hands of him** *when he got on drugs and refused to stop stealing from us.*
B: *Jesus! Tom was the smartest boy in class, but bad friends will undoubtedly drag us into trouble!*

Definition: to stop being involved or responsible for someone/something.

Measure your progress

<u>Fill in the gaps with the missing words;</u>

1. make sure you allow plenty of time to get .... your destination on time.

2. You've got to work 80 hour weeks if you want to get .... in your career.

3. Here's the .... of the matter, Bill. We feel like you're performance has been slipping recently.

4. Let's stop discussing trivial details and get to the ....

5. We're never going to get this project finished if you keep .... about instead of taking charge and making decisions!

6. You don't .... me as the type of person to do something like that.

7. James likes telling jokes and being the .... of attention at parties.

8. This necklace was handed .... to my mother by my grandmother.

9. Come on. Give me the wallet. Hand it ....!

10. Now that I'm rich, my parents wish they hadn't washed their .... of me when I refused to work for the family business.

Answers;

1. to   2. somewhere   3. heart   4. point   5. waffling
6. strike   7. center   8. down   9. over   10. hands

Chapter 6

Expressions (51 – 60)

51. hand/give/offer somebody something on a plate

Situation 1:

A: *See? We won the match hands down!*
B: *Not because of your efforts. The other team **gave that victory to you on a plate**.*

Situation 2:

A: *Mom, mom! I've finally got the job!*
B: *Congrats, sonny! But you **weren't handed the job on a plate**. Your father pulled some strings to employ you.*

Definition: to allow someone to get or win something very easily.

52. pull strings

Situation 1:

A: *I wonder why James wasn't sent to jail although he was the cause of that fatal accident!*
B: *His uncle might have **pulled strings** to get him out of trouble.*

Situation 2:

A: *I'm afraid we can't find a table at this hour.*
B: *I actually know a few people who work at the restaurant, so I'll see if I can **pull a few strings** and get a table.*

Definition: to secretly use the influence you have over important people in order to get something or to help someone.

53. one's hands are tied

Situation 1:

A: *I wish I could drive you to the airport but my car is broken right now so **my hands are tied**.*
B: *No big deal. I can call a cab.*

Situation 2:

A: *Can you please give me another copy of the dorm's key?*
B: *I wish I could, but **my hands are tied** because of the university regulations.*

Definition: not to be free to behave in the way that you would like; to be unable to act or do something.

54. have a hand in something

Situation 1:

A: *I assure you sir – I have nothing to do with what happened last night. I was out of town.*
B: *You were out of town, that's true. But we think you **had a hand in** planning the theft.*

Situation 2:

A: *Although I don't like to misjudge people, but deep down I know that Sally **has a hand in** the problem.*
B: *How do you know?*
A: *I overheard her talking on the phone and complaining about her colleagues.*

Definition: to be involved with something or have influence on something.

55. try one's hand at something

<u>Situation 1</u>:

A: *The summer break is just around the corner, and I'm bored already! Is there anything amusing we can do for a change?*
B: *Why don't we **try our hand at** Ping Pong (table tennis)? The city council are offering free classes on Saturdays.*

<u>Situation 2</u>:

A: *Why do you want to you change your field of study?*
B: *Well, I **tried my hand at** politics, but I found out that it wasn't my thing. Now, I'm considering pursuing a career in the arts instead.*

<u>Definition</u>: to try doing something for the first time.

56. need a hand

<u>Situation 1</u>:

A: *Oh geez, how do they put this thing together?*
B: ***Need a hand?***
A: *Yes, please.*

<u>Situation 2</u>:

A: *Do you **need a hand with** packing?*
B: *I can manage on my own, thanks.*

<u>Definition</u>: to need help with a task or chore (often used in a question as a set phrase).

<h1 style="text-align:center">57. in frustration</h1>

Situation 1:

A: *Did Mike take part in the contest?*
B: *He did, but after losing the second round, he quit **in frustration**.*

Situation 2:

A: *When Jessie heard about her daughter's illness. She beat her hands on the steering wheel **in frustration**.*
B: *Poor thing. I think we must be by her side in these hard times.*

Definition: having a feeling of anger or annoyance caused by being unable to do something.

<h1 style="text-align:center">58. in despair</h1>

Situation 1:

A: *What happened to Jenny when she was told about her dismissal?*
B: *She shook her head **in despair**, but said nothing.*

Situation 2:

A: *I haven't heard from Michael since last spring. How's he doing?*
B: *Not very well. Unfortunately, he was plunged **into despair** when his wife left him.*

Definition: without hope; to be losing hope.

59. unwavering

<u>Situation 1</u>:

A: *What makes your products live up to their reputation consistently?*
B: *In a word – our **unwavering** principles. We never compromise on our quality.*

<u>Situation 2</u>:

A: *John, what's the secret behind that constant smile of yours?*
B: *Well, I have **unwavering** faith that life is joyful and that we have the ability to bring cheer to others.*

<u>Definition</u>: (adjective) never changing or becoming weaker.

60. a set-up

<u>Situation 1</u>:

A: *How do I know this isn't a **set-up**?*
B: *You won't pay a penny until you have the boxes in your warehouse.*

<u>Situation 2</u>:

A: *The security guards say that they saw you enter the building at 7:00 p.m. So, stop playing games and tell me why did you steal the documents?*
B: *I swear didn't do it, this is **a set-up**!*

<u>Definition</u>: a scheme or trick intended to incriminate or deceive someone.

Measure your progress

<u>Fill in the gaps with the missing words;</u>

1. The experience you're seeking isn't going to be handed to you on a ....-, you know. You have to gain it.

2. I may be able to pull a few ....-if you need the document urgently.

3. It's so frustrating not to be able to help my brother financially but with two kids in college my hands are ....-.

4. Tell john about his girlfriend's message yourself. I don't want to ....-a hand in his personal affairs.

5. Sally decided to ....-her hand at writing poetry and discovered she was good at it.

6. I think Matthew might ....-a hand with his maths homework.

7. In ....-, Anne quit her cashier job after several months for a more lucrative position as a bank teller.

8. Sam hanged himself in ....-over problems in his marriage.

9. She has been encouraged by the ....-support of her family.

10. When drugs were found in her luggage, she claimed it was a ....-up.

Answers;

1. plate   2. strings   3. tied   4. have   5. try
6. need   7. frustration   8. despair   9. unwavering   10. set

Chapter 7

Expressions (61 – 70)

61. the ball is in someone's court

Situation 1:

A: *I filled out the form and applied it,* **now the ball's in your court.**
B: *Consider it done! I've already pulled some strings for you to get the position.*

Situation 2:

A: *Did you make up with Mike?*
B: *Not really. I've sent them a message of apology but he hasn't responded yet.*
A: *Well,* **the ball's in his court,** *then.*

Definition: it is someone's responsibility to take the next action or decision in a situation; it is time for someone to deal with a problem or make a decision, because other people have already done as much as they can.

62. Consider it done

Situation 1:

A: *Anne, I need you to email this letter to all departments today.*
B: **Consider it done,** *boss!*

Situation 2:

A: *Hey, Bill. Could you get that flat tire replaced for me?*
B: **Consider it done,** *dad!*
A: *Good boy. I know I can count on you.*

Definition: your request is fulfilled directly (used to say that you will do a particular task immediately).

63. on/by someone's side

Situation 1:

A: *I went to withdraw cash for our project, but the teller said the funds would not be available until further notice. I'm afraid I won't able to get my money.*
B: *Never mind. You have the law **on your side** if the bank is acting inappropriately.*

Situation 2:

A: *I'm sorry if I've hurt your feelings, honey. I was on edge for the past few days!*
B: *I don't mind you taking things out on me a bit, but I just wanted to let you know that I am here for you. I am **by your side**.*

Definition: to be supportive of someone.

64. time is on someone's side

Situation 1:

A: *We don't have to rush the sale of our assets. They're rising in value day by day. I mean we've **got time on our side**.*
B: *Good point. The longer we wait, the more they will be worth.*

Situation 2:

A: *Hey, guys. We need to get this report complete by 4:00. No need to remind you that **time isn't on our side**!*
B: *No problem, sir. Consider it done!*

Definition: someone has enough time to do something; the more that time passes, the more somebody will be helped: not having to worry about how long something will take.

65. take something out on someone

Situation 1:

A: *Look, Dave. I'm really tired of you **taking your frustration out on me**. Why don't you take some time off and go on a vacation for a change?*
B: *Yeah, you're right. I could do with some relaxation.*

Situation 2:

A: *Why did you treat that customer like dirt? It's unlike, Danny!*
B: *He's Mike's cousin.*
B: *I know you're mad at Mike but you don't have to **take out your anger on his cousin**!*

Definition: to treat someone badly because you are upset or angry, even if they have done nothing wrong.

66. treat someone like dirt

Situation 1:

A: *There's a vacant position at Bill's company if you're interested.*
B: *Fat chance. I won't work for Bill even if I'm paid a million. He **treats all his employees like dirt**.*

Situation 2:

A: *Look at this post. Diana says she's going on a trip to Istanbul with her husband.*
B: *Not impressed! I don't know why this man stays with her - she **treats him like dirt**.*

Definition: to treat someone with a complete lack of respect.

<h1 style="text-align:center">67. fat chance</h1>

<u>Situation 1</u>:

A: *You want Bill to give up his seat?* ***Fat chance.***
B: *Just wait and see!*

<u>Situation 2</u>:

A: ***Fat chance*** *I'm going to the party. I'm on a diet and I might not be able to resist the temptation of the chocolate cake.*
B: *Come on, Sarah. If you do eat a piece of chocolate cake, it won' be the end of the world.*

<u>Definition</u>: very little or no possibility (used to say that you certainly do not think that something is likely to happen).

<h1 style="text-align:center">68. Just (you) wait and see</h1>

<u>Situation 1</u>:

A: *Do you think they liked my presentation?*
B: *Of course, they did. I'm sure they'll call you back,* ***just you wait and see!***

<u>Situation 2</u>:

A: *Suzan is for sure mad at me after I made a fool out of her in the meeting.*
B: *She's mad as a hornet. She'll make you regret the day you ever crossed her,* ***just you wait and see!***

<u>Definition</u>: Be patient until you see what happens (used to emphasize a threat, warning or promise).

69. come what may

Situation 1:

A: *You'd better keep this for yourself. If Joe learns that you're the one who smashed the screen, he'll be mad at you.*
B: *I'll tell the truth, **come what may**.*

Situation 2:

A: *Are you sure you'll close the deal now?*
B: ***Come what may**, I won't change my mind.*

Definition: no matter what might happen; whatever happens.

70. misjudge

Situation 1:

A: *Sorry, Tom. I thought you weren't going to support me, but I **misjudged** you.*
B: *Never mind, buddy! I'm by your side, come what may!*

Situation 2:

A: *Uncle Steven offered to pay off our debts with no strings attached. Can you imagine?*
B: *What a very kind thing to do - I've been **misjudging** him all these years.*

Definition: to form an unfair or wrong judgment about a person or thing; to be mistaken in your judgment.

Measure your progress

Fill in the gaps with the missing words;

1. I've helped him in every way I can – the ball's in his
.... now.

2. Our team is working on the proposed layout, so ....
it done.

3. Come what may, we'll always stand by your ....

4. Although Anne failed the exam, ... is on her side;
she is young enough to take it again next year.

5. I know you've had a bad day, but you don't have to take it
.... on me!

6. Gone are the days when we were treated as key workers and now
we are being treated like ....

7. A higher school team would have a fat .... beating a
strong college team.

8. I'm not going to tell you who else I've invited - you'll just have to
.... and see.

9. I knew he'd be able to take care of himself, come
.... may.

10. Sophie shouldn't have shouted at her fiancé. She totally
.... the situation and behaved inappropriately.

Answers;

1. court   2. consider   3. side   4. time   5. out
6. dirt   7. chance   8. wait   9. what   10. misjudged

Chapter 8

Expressions (71 – 80)

<h1 style="text-align:center">71. capture the moment</h1>

<u>Situation 1</u>:

A: *How did you manage to get this nice scene on film?*
B: *I tried to* **capture the moment** *when you're in the middle of the ceremony.*

<u>Situation 2</u>:

A: *With the widespread availability of high-resolution cell phones cameras, most people have the potential to be professional photographers.*
B: *That's right. Personally, I use my phone camera to* **capture the moment** *– I pull out my phone and take photos three or four times a day.*

<u>**Definition**</u>: to be more present and mindful during the point in time at which something happens.

<h1 style="text-align:center">72. show of hands</h1>

<u>Situation 1</u>:

A: *No one wants to play soccer today?*
B: *I guess not. I asked for a* **show of hands**, *and no one was interested.*

<u>Situation 2</u>:

A: *Class, we'll select the volunteers by* ***a show of hands***. *Who wants to plant trees?*
B: *Sorry, sir. I'd love to join this group but I have to help my father with the office renovation at the weekend.*
A: *Ok, Joe. You may volunteer for recycling on weekdays.*

<u>**Definition**</u>: a display of raised hands [in a group of people] that can be counted for the purpose of votes or surveys.

73. stand one's ground

Situation 1:

A: *Everyone approved the policy changes. Why did you **stand your ground**?*
B: *Although I might be looked upon as an uncooperative team player, I feel this new policy is like a scam. I refuse to give in – come what may.*

Situation 2:

A: *All the boys ran when they saw the coyote except Mike.*
B: *He reminds me of his grandfather. A man who used to **stand his ground** in the face of adversity.*

Definition: not to run away from a situation, but face it bravely; to refuse to change your opinion or give in to an argument.

74. double-cross

Situation 1:

A: *Do you really trust that hoodlum?*
B: *Why shouldn't I? I get my goods delivered and he gets his cash – it's a win-win.*
A: *I don't know, but they say that he would even **double-cross** his own mother.*

Situation 2:

A: *Simon, I know you're a swindler. I'm warning you - if you **double-cross** me, I'll kill you.*
B: *I swear I won't. Everything will turn out just fine.*

Definition: to cheat someone, especially after you have agreed to do something dishonest with them; to trick or cheat someone who trusts you.

75. tend /attend to someone/something

Situation 1:

A: *Are you leaving already? You've just come, buddy!*
B: *I have some urgent business to **attend to.***

Situation 2:

A: *The final exams are just around the corner. You must **tend to your studies**, sonny.*
B: *I will - and I will make you proud of me, mom. I promise!*

Definition: to take care of the needs of someone or something; to respond to a request or demand from someone or something.

76. tend to do something

Situation 1:

A: *I heard that Jessie and her brothers are fighting over their inherited property.*
B: *I **tend not to believe** rumors like these until I see some actual evidence.*

Situation 2:

A: *I feel that I'm out of luck these days. I've lost half of my money investing in digital currency.*
B: *Enough of this foolishness, Mark. Every time you make a bad decision, you say it's bad luck. There's no such thing as bad luck. People **tend to** confuse bad decisions with bad luck.*

Definition: to have a tendency or disposition to do or be something; to be inclined to do something; to be likely to happen or to have a particular characteristic or effect.

77. confuse with

Situation 1:

A: *Hey, Derek! How's it going?*
B: *Oh, I'm not Derek. I'm afraid you have **confused me with** my brother.*

Situation 2:

A: *Have you sorted out the books?*
B: *I did!*
A: *Seriously! You've apparently **confused the old ones with the new ones**.*

Definition: to mix someone up with someone else; to mistake someone or something for someone or something else.

78. within reason

Situation 1:

A: *I will do everything I can to make this dream a reality—**within reason**, of course.*
B: *Good for you, Bob. That's the spirit!*

Situation 2:

A: *Dad, now that I passed the exam with flying scores – don't I deserve a reward?*
B: *Certainly. Choose any present you like **within reason** of course.*

Definition: fair or reasonable and not too extreme; within the limits of what is acceptable and possible.

79. couldn't agree more

<u>Situation 1</u>:

A: *Regardless of what topics we discuss here, we need to allow enough time to each other. I mean we should speak within reason.*
B: *I **couldn't agree more**. I'm glad to hear you say that.*

<u>Situation 2</u>:

A: *Bill's such a lousy mechanic. He doesn't even have the tools!*
B: *I **couldn't agree more**!*

<u>Definition</u>: to strongly or completely agree.

80. flat out

<u>Situation 1</u>:

A: *Steven, you owe me a hundred bucks. I want them back now!*
B: *I can tell you **flat out**, no way am I paying that money.*

<u>Situation 2</u>:

A: *Do you think I'm an idiot to believe what Joe says. He just **flat out** lied to all of us.*
B: *I couldn't agree more!*

<u>Definition</u>: in a very clear and direct way; without hesitation or reservation.

Measure your progress

<u>**Fill in the gaps with the missing words;**</u>

1. John will capture the .... with his eight year old artistic camera. He always has his camera handy to preserve family memories.

2. Let's have a .... of hands. Who's in favor of the proposal?

3. Despite my opponent's size, I managed to stand my .... during the fight.

4. He double-................................ the rest of the gang and disappeared with all the money.

5. You really need to .... to the lawn—it's getting pretty overgrown!

6. Doctors these days .... to be more open-minded about alternative medicine.

7. People are always .... me with my sister because we look so much alike.

8. We can wear anything we like to the office, ... reason.

9. Bob says you manipulated him into going to the party, and I couldn't agree ....

10. He asked if I would join them and I told him .... out 'No'.

Answers;
1. moment   2. show   3. ground   4. crossed   5. attend
6. tend   7. confusing   8. within   9. more   10. flat

Chapter 9

Expressions (81 – 90)

81. scouting trip

Situation 1:

A: *Where have you been, George? You scared the heck out of me when I didn't find you in the hut!*
B: *I went on a **scouting trip**, thinking I might get track of something.*

Situation 2:

A: *Did you say you saw a coyote? When was that?*
B: *When we were returning from the **scouting trip** on which you sent us to locate new water sources.*

Definition: a journey taken to gain information; a journey organized just to explore a place or make sure something or someone is there.

82. reverse/turn the tide

Situation 1:

A: *We still have the option of replacing the defense players. Do you think it's useful at this point?*
B: *Very useful, and can definitely **turn the tide** of the match.*

Situation 2:

A: *What steps can be taken to **reverse the tide** of plastic flowing around the world?*
B: *People should be encouraged to reuse their plastic bags and recycle as much as they can.*

Definition: to change or reverse something dramatically; to cause a reversal in the direction of events.

83. get under someone's skin

<u>**Situation 1**</u>:

A: *You didn't have to blow up at Dania like that – I felt like two cents!*
B: *She deserved it. She made a comment about a friend of mine that* **got under my skin**. *I felt that if I didn't say something, I would walk around angry all day.*

<u>**Situation 2**</u>:

A: *Take it easy, Bob. Why should you get upset each time you meet the boss?*
B: *This man is really good at* **getting under my skin** *with his constant reminding.*

<u>**Definition**</u>: to irritate or upset someone; to make someone angry.

84. blow up at someone

<u>**Situation 1**</u>:

A: *You don't seem to be on good terms with your roommate?*
B: *Yeah, she* **blew up at me** *last Saturday for no reason. We haven't been talking to each other since then.*

<u>**Situation 2**</u>:

A: *I'm sorry that I* **blew up at you** *like that—work is so frustrating right now that I have no patience left when I get home.*
B: *It's OK, darling. I don't mind if you take your frustration out on me as long as it gives you some relief.*

<u>**Definition**</u>: to become suddenly very angry and shout at someone.

85. get upset

<u>Situation 1</u>:

A: *Jesus! I spilled coffee on my dress and the premiere will start in five minutes.*
B: *Don't **get upset**, honey - there's only a little stain on it.*

<u>Situation 2</u>:

A: *Come on, Sam. You didn't study at all. Why **get upset** just because you got a bad mark?*
B: *Because my mom is gonna skin my alive.*

<u>Definition</u>: to become or to feel worried, unhappy, or angry.

86. on good terms (with someone)

<u>Situation 1</u>:

A: *Are you sure Michael didn't get upset during the debate?*
B: *No, not at all. We shook hands and parted **on good terms**.*

<u>Situation 2</u>:

A: *Although Joe's parents disinherited him, he remained **on good terms with them.***
B: *Good for him. He's one of a kind!*

<u>Definition</u>: to have a good, friendly, etc. relationship with someone: if two people are on good terms or on friendly terms, they are friendly with each other.

87. blow off steam

Situation 1:

A: *Why did you leave so early?*
B: *Jerry's nagging voice got under my skin. I was getting more and more frustrated, thus, I decided to run home to **blow off some steam**.*

Situation 2:

A: *Thanks, buddy. I really feel better after I opened up to you.*
B: *You're always welcome. Call me any time you need to **blow off some steam**. I'm here for you, buddy.*

Definition: to get rid of pent-up energy or strong emotion; to do or say something that helps you to get rid of strong feelings or energy.

88. open up (to someone)

Situation 1:

A: *Jeff's been leading a reclusive life recently. Don't you think?*
B: *I've been trying to get him to **open up** a bit, but he just likes to keep things to himself.*

Situation 2:

A: *Hey, mom. I'd like to tell you something, but promise me you won't get upset?*
B: *What's it?*
A: *My sister **opened up** and told me she's very unhappy in her marriage.*
B: *Is she? Oh, goodness! This girl is gonna send me to the loony bin!*

Definition: to talk about what you feel and think; to become less shy and more willing to communicate.

89. take to heart

Situation 1:

A: *Bill is determined to leave school and work as a waiter. I talked to him but he was adamant.*
B: *I'll ask Jack to talk some sense into him. Bill is on good terms with Jack and takes what he says to heart.*

Situation 2:

A: *Mike blew up at me just because I asked him to pick up his room!*
B: *Your brother has been through a lot recently. You shouldn't* **take everything he says to heart**.

Definition: to take something (criticism or advice) seriously.

90. blow one's top

Situation 1:

A: *Why is the car dented? Did you have an accident? My father will* **blow his top** *when he sees what happened to his car.*
B: *It wasn't my fault. A dog appeared out of nowhere and smashed into it.*

Situation 2:

A: *It was unusual for Matt to* **blow his top** *in public.*
B: *His flight was cancelled at the last minute and he lost a million dollars as a result. I'd have lost my mind if I had been in his place as well.*

Definition: to lose one's temper; to become extremely angry.

Measure your progress

<u>Fill in the gaps with the missing words;</u>

1. The film revolves around an aging baseball scout whose daughter joins him on a .... trip.

2. They had won the battle and turned the .... of the war, but each of them felt cold inside.

3. I've noticed that little things have been getting under my .... lately – things that shouldn't upset me.

4. My mum blew .... at my dad for keeping me up so late.

5. Pull yourself together. It's ridiculous to get .... about such a silly little thing.

6. We have always been on good .... with our neighbors. We never fight over anything.

7. Don't apologize for shouting at them; it does you good to blow off .... occasionally.

8. Everyone cried when the speaker .... up and told us how he lost his daughter to cancer.

9. Had he taken the advice to ...., he wouldn't have got in trouble.

10. When my dad found out I had failed the exams, he just .... his top.

Answers;

1. scouting   2. tide   3. skin   4. up   5. upset
6. terms   7. steam   8. opened   9. heart   10. blew

Chapter 10

Expressions (91 – 100)

91. pull oneself together

Situation 1:

A: *Oh, no. I don't believe I failed. I've totally screwed up!*
B: *Stop crying and **pull yourself together!** Trust me, Matt, failing a class isn't the end of the world.*

Situation 2:

A: *Come on, Jack! Put on your jacket and let's go home. I can't stand Jessie's disrespect anymore.*
B: *But we're here to celebrate your niece's graduation not to argue with Jessie. Now, **pull yourself together**, honey, and please don't get upset about such a silly little thing.*

Definition: to become calm and behave normally again after being angry or upset; recover control of one's emotions.

92. hoodlum

Situation 1:

A: *Can we take the suspects to the office for interrogation, sir?*
B: *Why is that?*
A: *Ms. Thomson doesn't want "those little **hoodlums**," as she calls them, in her house any longer than necessary.*

Situation 2:

A: *What's wrong, Sue? Why are you crying? Are you okay?*
B: *I'm not okay. Bill had those hoodlums who robbed us here for the party.*
A: *Calm down, sweetie. I need you to **pull yourself together** now. I asked him to do so for some purpose.*

Definition: a criminal, esp. one who is a member of a group; a violent criminal or troublemaker; a hooligan or gangster.

93. an honest mistake

Situation 1:

A: *Unless I miss my guess, Mathew sold us out by sharing the emails with the police. Our names are mentioned there.*

B: *It must've been an **honest mistake**. Mathew would never try to double-cross us.*

Situation 2:

A: *I'm the one who switched off the lights and caused all the mess, but it was an **honest mistake**. I swear.*

B: *Common sense says an **honest mistake** must be followed by an honest apology.*

A: *Yeah, you owe my an apology, guys. I'm really sorry and I'm willing to do what it takes to make up for my mistake.*

Definition: a mistake that wasn't made deliberately, or had no bad intent; a mistake made by a person with no wrong intention.

94. sell someone out

Situation 1:

A: *I shouldn't have trusted you to keep my secret. I can't believe that you **sold me out**!*

B: *I assure you it was an honest mistake. Someone must have overheard me while I was talking to you on the bus.*

Situation 2:

A: *The hoodlums caught Joe while we were on a scouting trip to find out where they gather. What if he gave away our whereabouts to them?*

B: *That's unlikely to happen. Joe is a reliable person. He will never **sell out** his friends.*

Definition: to betray someone for a personal benefit; to give up support for a person or belief for money or personal advantage; to reveal damaging information about someone.

95. tear/rip (someone or something) to shreds (1)

<u>Situation 1</u>:

A: *Look at your shirt -* ***it's torn to shreds****!*
B: *Yeah, I was lying under the car trying to repair it.*

<u>Situation 2</u>:

A: *Break it up, boys – you've **torn each other to shreds***!
B: *I won't stop unless he returns my pencil case.*

<u>Definition</u>: to damage someone or something badly.

96. tear/rip (someone or something) to shreds (2)

<u>Situation 1</u>:

A: *Did the thesis committee go hard on you during the discussion?*
B: *Well, they **ripped me to shreds** for some punctuation mistakes. They're very precise, I'm telling you.*

<u>Situation 2</u>:

A: *Do you know anything about this course we're about to attend?*
B: *Well, one Facebook reviewer **tore it to shreds**, but I still think it's going to be fine because I know the teacher.*

<u>Definition</u>: to criticize (someone or something) in a very harsh or angry way.

97. revolve around/about (1)

Situation 1:

A: *Sally failed the driving test because she didn't know that the car wheels are **revolving about** an axis.*
B: *That comes as no surprise to me. She's doesn't know the first thing about cars.*

Situation 2:

A: *Does the sun **revolve around** the earth or the other way round?*
B: *What a silly question! A 5-year-old kid can answer it.*

Definition: to move around (something) in a path that is similar to a circle; to turn around or rotate, as on an axis.

98. revolve around/about (2)

Situation 1:

A: *What's this movie about?*
B: *It **revolves around** people holding guns on other people.*

Situation 2:

A: *Did you attend the meeting?*
B: *I did. It largely **revolved about** rumors of potential pay raise.*

Definition: to have (someone or something) as a main subject or interest.

99. behind the scenes

<u>Situation 1</u>:

A: *David has finally retired! This is the best news ever!*
B: *You don't have to be so excited about it. He'll remain active **behind the scenes**. He's the boss's step-brother, you know.*

<u>Situation 2</u>:

A: *Thanks for sharing that video. It's an exciting opportunity to learn what goes on **behind the scenes**.*
B: *Don't mention it!*

<u>Definition</u>: secretly (if something happens behind the scenes, it happens without most people knowing about it).

100. watch oneself

<u>Situation 1</u>:

A: ***Watch yourself** in the area; there are lots of hoodlums.*
B: *Don't worry about me. If any of them crossed my path, they'd curse the day they were born.*

<u>Situation 2</u>:

A: *I'm very skillful at using sharp knives. Look, I can swirl it in the air!*
B: *You better **watch yourself** for you will get hurt.*

<u>Definition</u>: to be cautious; to be very careful in one's actions or speech, so as not to do or say something harmful or offensive.

Measure your progress

<u>Fill in the gaps with the missing words;</u>

1. After that frightening episode, it took her a while to pull herself
....

2. The detective kept both .... separate and talked to each one quietly so the other could not hear.

3. It was an .... mistake! How was I to know that you wouldn't want me to send that box?

4. The company had put a lot of trust on him, but he .... them out by leaking confidential information to the competitors.

5. My trousers were torn to .... when I fell off my bike.

6. I hear John's bosses .... him to shreds at his annual performance review.

7. As we know, electrons revolve .... the nucleus, or center of an atom.

8. The conversation .... around childcare problems.

9. I choose to be a back-office employee because I prefer to work quietly .... the scenes.

10. .... yourself up on the roof. You may fall if you make any wrong move.

Answers;

1. together   2. hoodlums   3. honest   4. sold   5. shreds
6. tore   7. about/around   8. revolved   9. behind   10. Watch

List of Phrases

Chapter (1)

know the drill
you name it
drive safely
live up to one's reputation
live up to (one's) end of the bargain
live up to something
kick oneself
good point
get someone through something
get through to someone (1)

Chapter (2)

get through (to someone) (2)
make one's point
think ill of someone/something
think highly of someone/something
go/get nowhere
put one's heart into something
overthink
you never can tell
you never know
you may well ask

Chapter (3)

guesswork
rub shoulders with
hands down (1)
hands down (2)
feel cheap
speak someone's language

accidents (will) happen
overhear
keep on something
keep on at someone

Chapter (4)

it's unlike you
Says who?
hands-off approach
first-hand experience
at hand
get to do something
get someone to do something
get to something
get to someone (1)
get to someone (2)

Chapter (5)

get to somewhere
get somewhere
the heart of the matter
get/come to the point
waffle
strike someone as something
the center of attention
hand something down
hand it over
wash one's hand of

Chapter (6)

hand/give/offer somebody something on a plate
pull strings
one's hands are tied
have a hand in something
try one's hand at something
need a hand
in frustration
in despair
unwavering
a set-up

Chapter (7)

the ball is in someone's court
Consider it done
on/by someone's side
time is on someone's side
take something out on someone
treat someone like dirt
fat chance
Just (you) wait and see
come what may
misjudge

Chapter (8)

capture the moment
show of hands
stand one's ground
double-cross
tend /attend to someone/something
tend to do something
confuse with
within reason
couldn't agree more

flat out

Chapter (9)
scouting trip
reverse/turn the tide
get under someone's skin
blow up at someone
get upset
on good terms (with someone)
blow off steam
open up (to someone)
take to heart
blow one's top

Chapter (10)
pull oneself together
hoodlum
an honest mistake
sell someone out
tear/rip (someone or something) to shreds (1)
tear/rip (someone or something) to shreds (2)
revolve around/about (1)
revolve around/about (2)
behind the scenes
watch oneself

Other works by the author

Phrasal Verbs (Advanced) The Comprehensive Collection: 1060 Common Phrasal Verbs with Plenty of Examples & Synonyms
https://www.amazon.com/dp/B09NGYYCH8

ADVANCED ENGLISH: Idioms, Phrasal Verbs, Vocabulary and Phrases: 700 Expressions of Academic Language
https://www.amazon.com/dp/B07RTGWH5X

Advanced English Collocations & Phrases in Dialogues: Master English Collocations with the Aid of Functional Dialogues once and for all https://www.amazon.com/dp/B086JYB24J

Advanced English Collocations & Phrases in Dialogues (2)
https://www.amazon.com/dp/B0B752S8S4

Advanced English Conversations (1): Speak English Like a Native
https://www.amazon.com/dp/B09PLD4GHN

Advanced English Conversations (2): Speak English Like a Native
https://www.amazon.com/dp/B089YTQPTV

Advanced English Conversations (3); Speak English Like a Native
https://www.amazon.com/dp/B0B2SD8TNF

Advanced English Conversation in Dialogues
https://www.amazon.com/dp/B0BBL1HB24

American Idioms and Idiomatic Phrases In Use (1)
https://www.amazon.com/dp/B0BH2W3MB9

TOEFL VOCABULARY (Adjectives)
https://www.amazon.com/dp/B0BD9FR6X2

TOEFL VOCABULARY (NOUNS)
https://www.amazon.com/dp/B0BK9S22RF

Daily English Expressions: Speak English Like a Native
https://www.amazon.com/dp/B0BLHXZJL8

Daily English Expressions (book - 2): Speak English Like a Native
https://www.amazon.com/dp/B0BMYRBJZF

Daily English Expressions (book - 3): Speak English Like a Native
https://www.amazon.com/dp/B0BNGPCVNQ

Daily English Expressions (Book - 4) : Speak English Like a Native
https://www.amazon.com/dp/B0BP5CPPNX

Daily English Expressions (Book - 5) : Speak English Like a Native
https://www.amazon.com/dp/B0BQFMGN6J

Daily English Expressions (Book - 6): Speak English Like a Native
https://www.amazon.com/dp/B0BRWLGYT9

Daily English Expressions (Book - 7): Speak English Like a Native
https://www.amazon.com/dp/B0BSR71WZH

Daily English Expressions (Book - 8): Speak English Like a Native
https://www.amazon.com/dp/B0BTMLFVCN

Daily English Expressions (Book - 9): Speak English Like a Native
https://www.amazon.com/dp/B0BVP8F7N1

Daily English Expressions (Book - 10): Speak English Like a Native
https://www.amazon.com/dp/B0BXBC5L52

Spoken English Phrases (book - 1): Speak English Like a Native

https://www.amazon.com/dp/B0C18Z2X52

Spoken English Phrases (book - 2): Speak English Like a Native

https://www.amazon.com/dp/B0C18X5T1Y

Spoken English Phrases (book - 3): Speak English Like a Native
https://www.amazon.com/dp/B0C3B75NZJ

Spoken English Phrases (book - 4): Speak English Like a Native
https://www.amazon.com/dp/B0C7CM43XC

Spoken English Phrases (book - 5): Speak English Like a Native
https://www.amazon.com/dp/B0C9WZ4S93